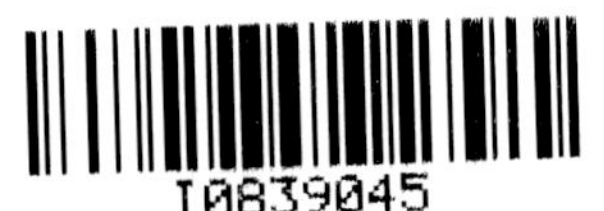

Coloring book for adults and kids amazing panda image for design

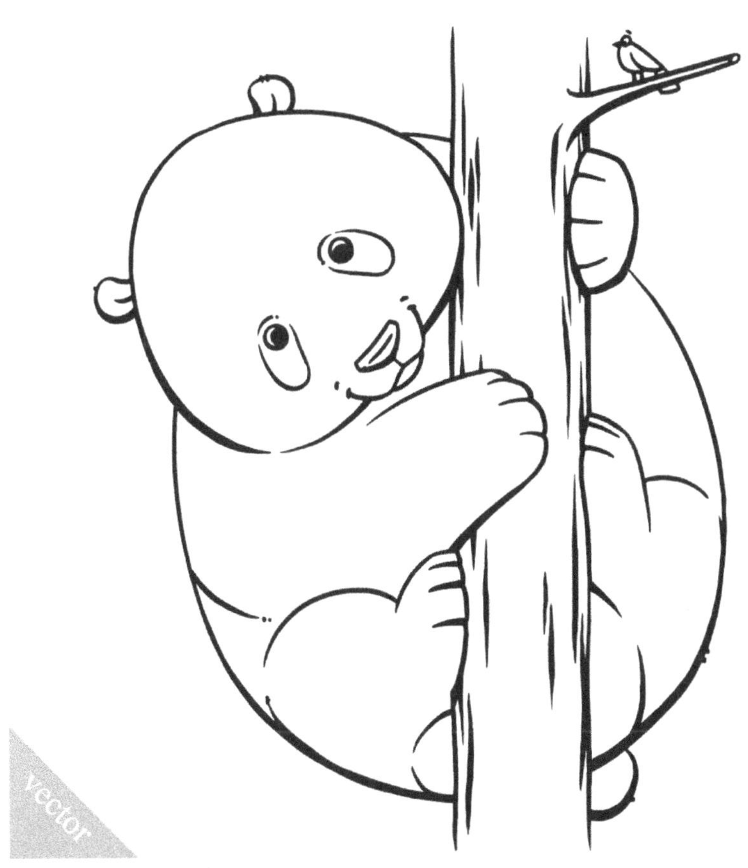

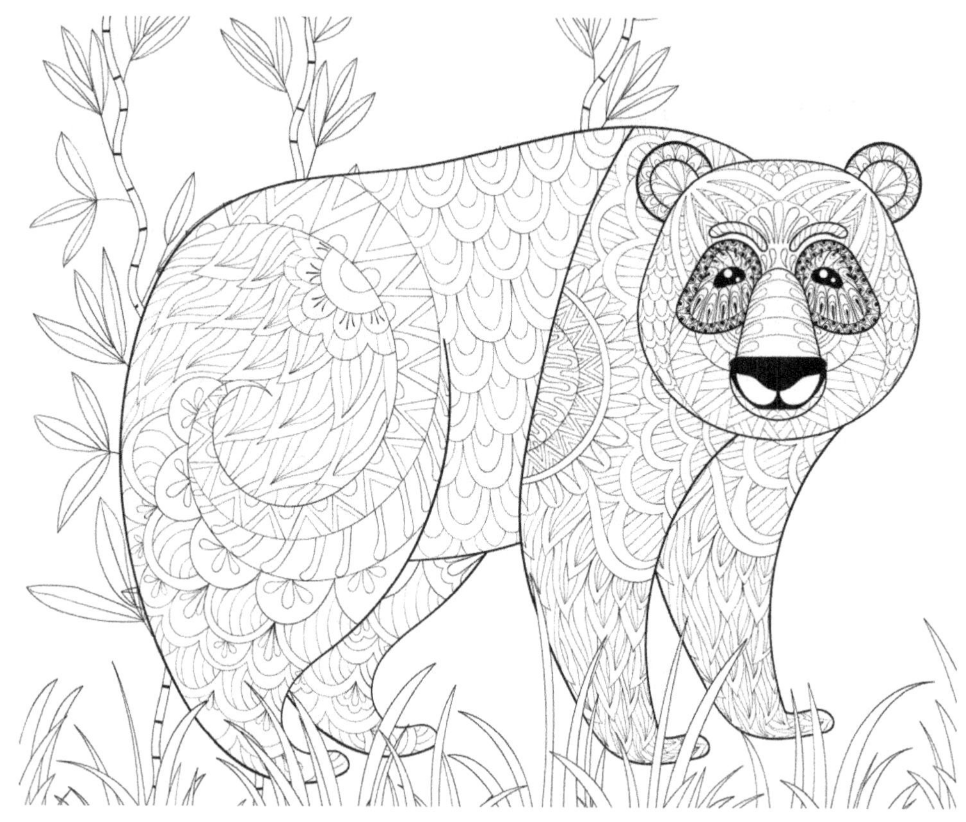

This coloring book is belongs to

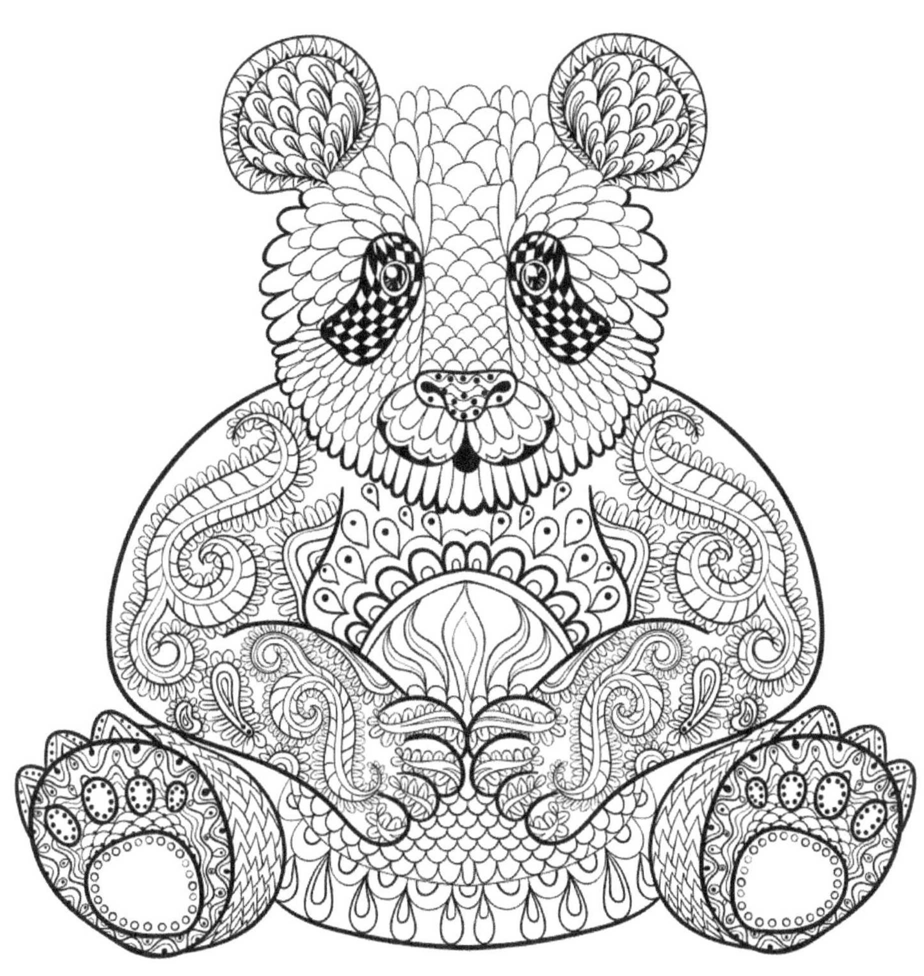

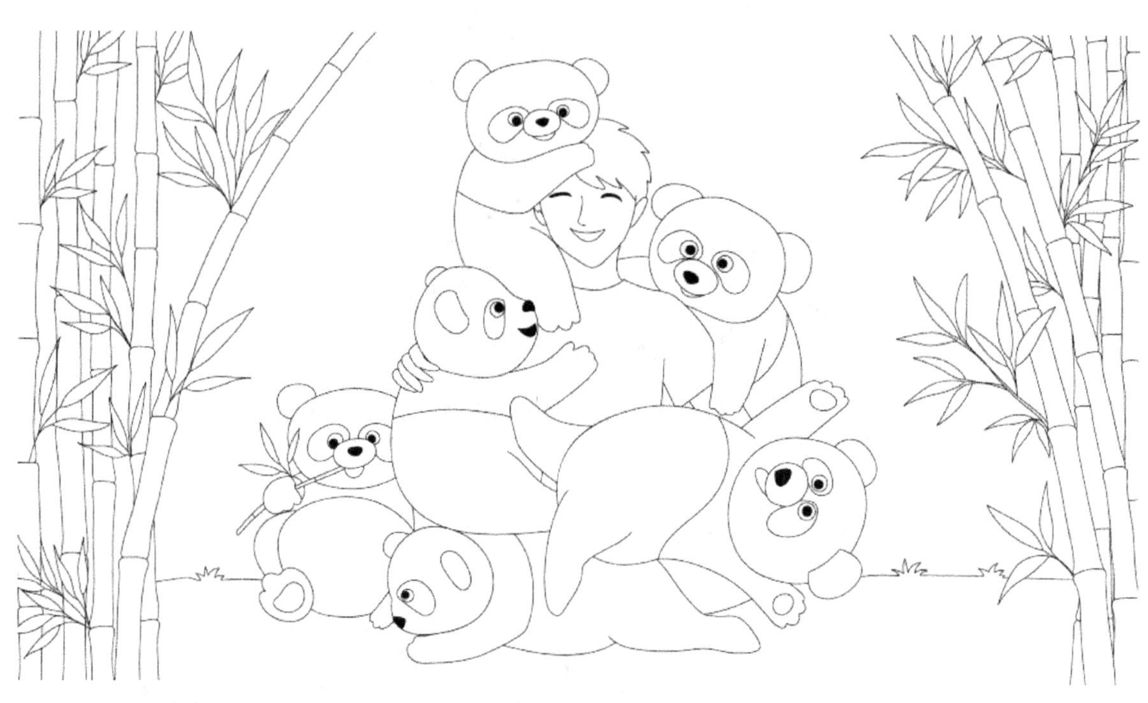

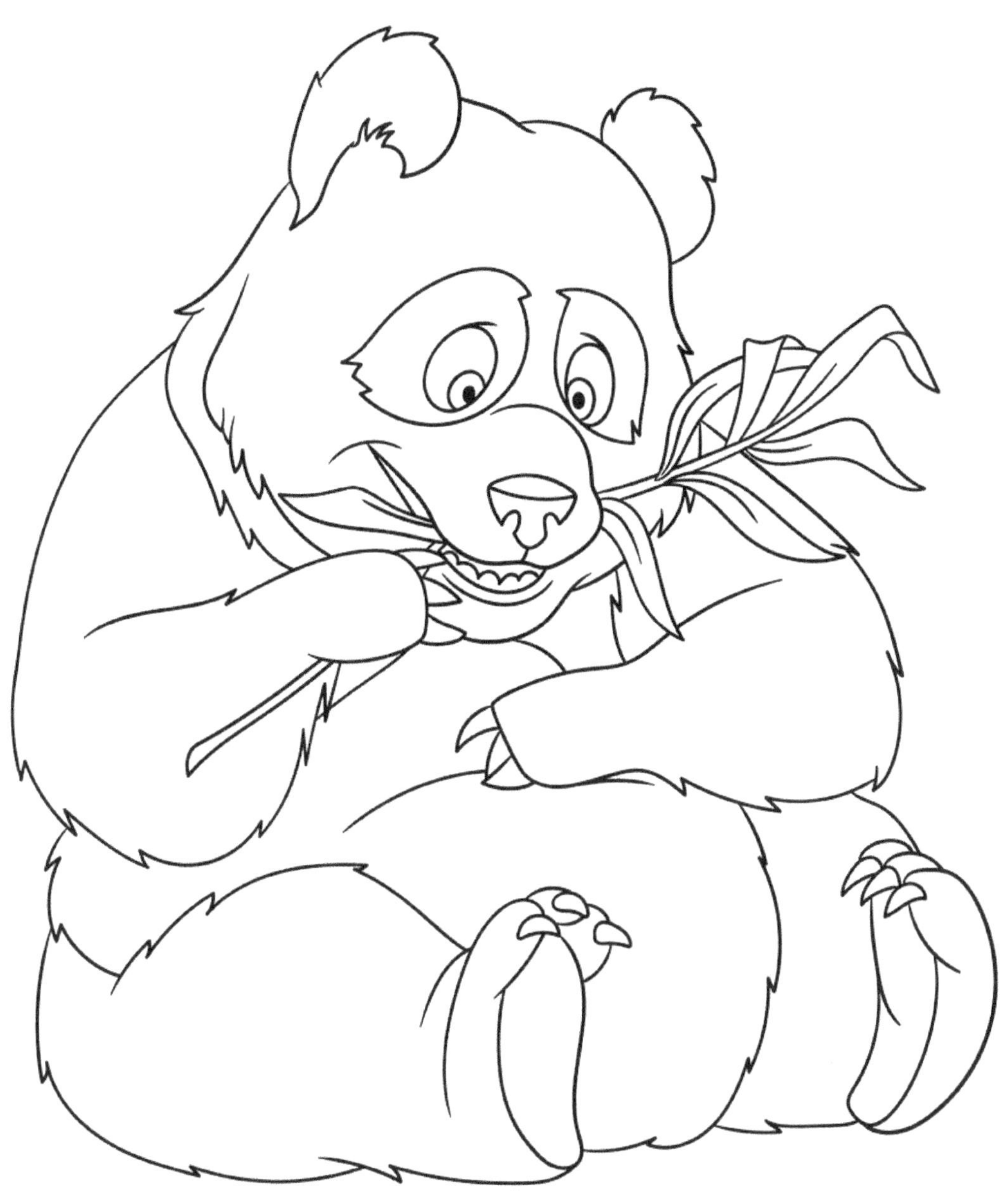

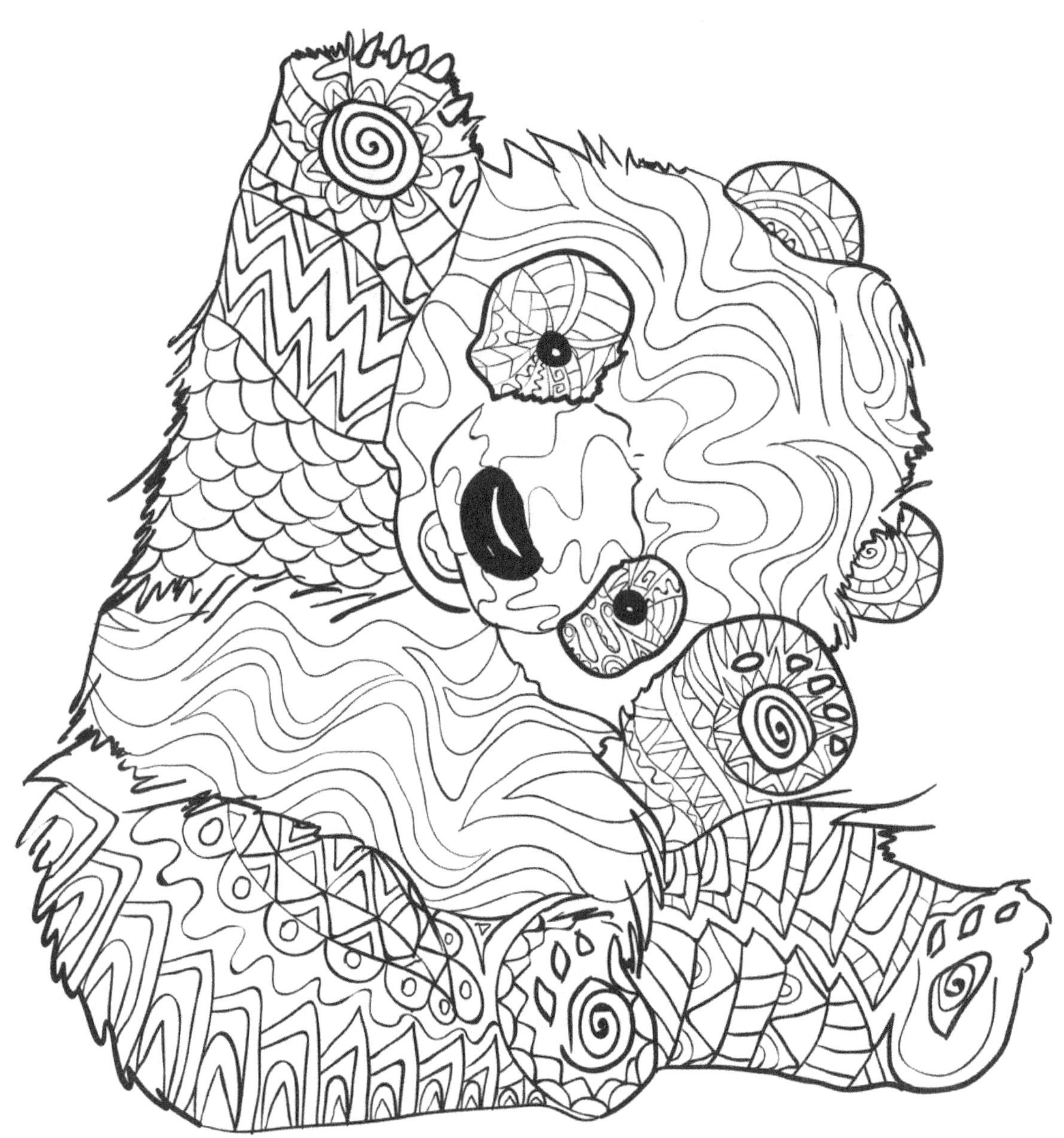

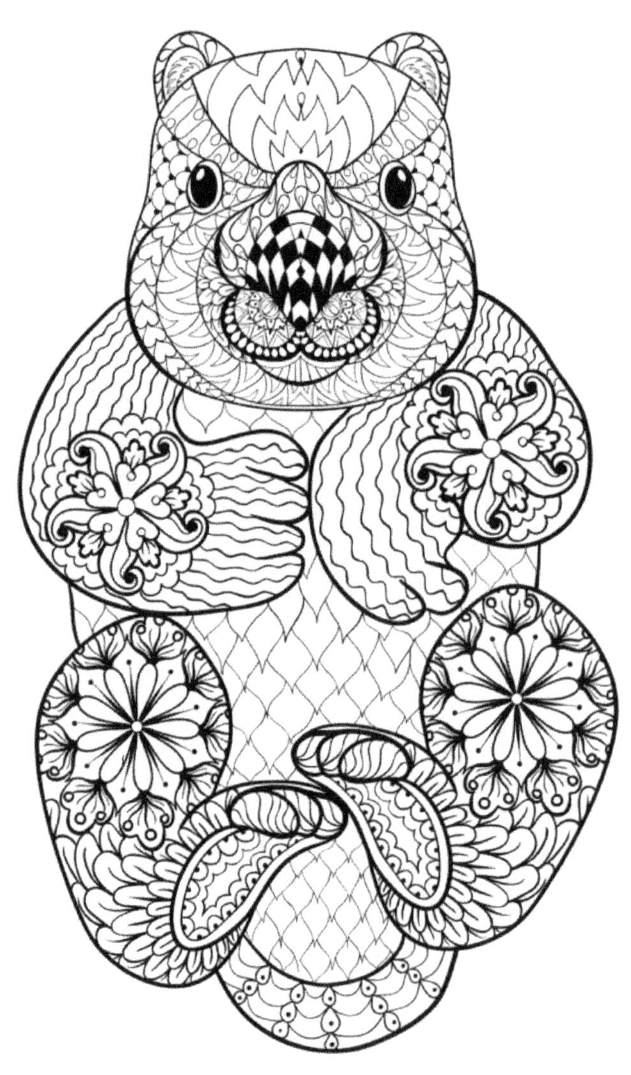

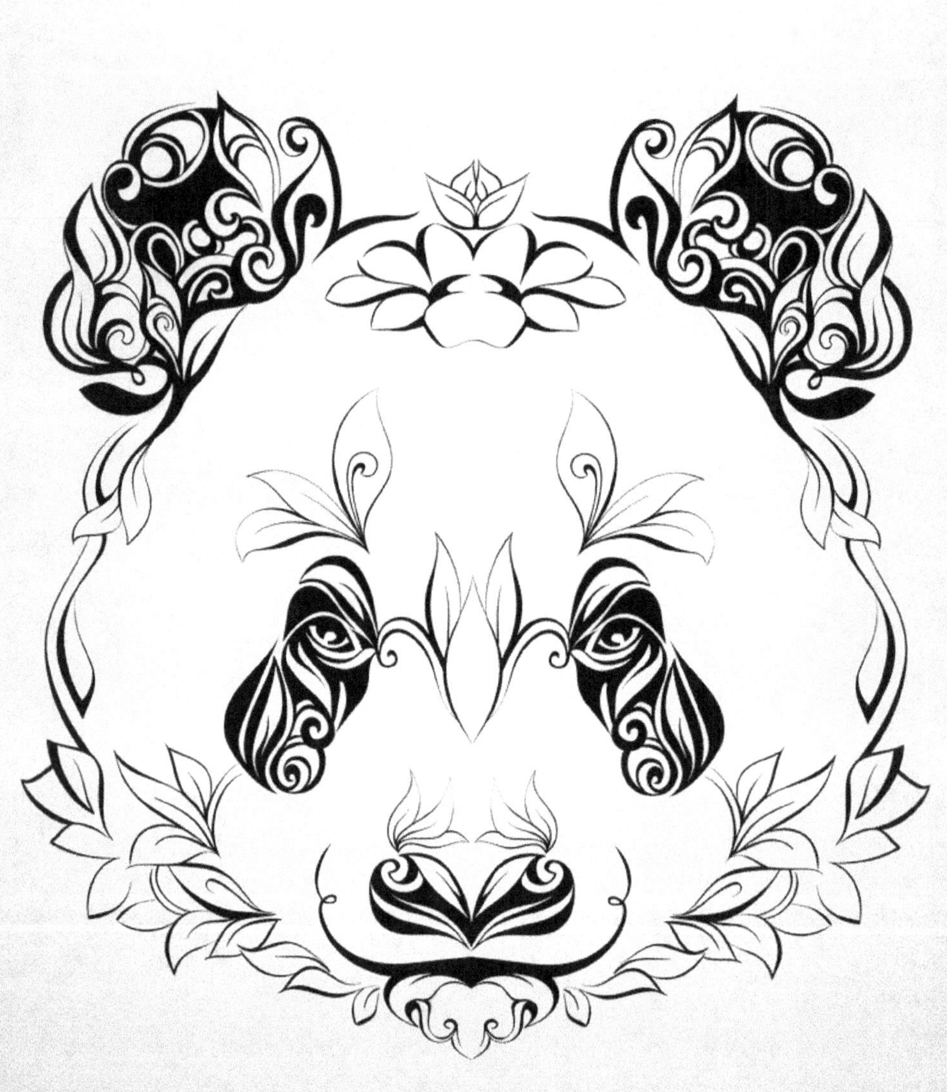

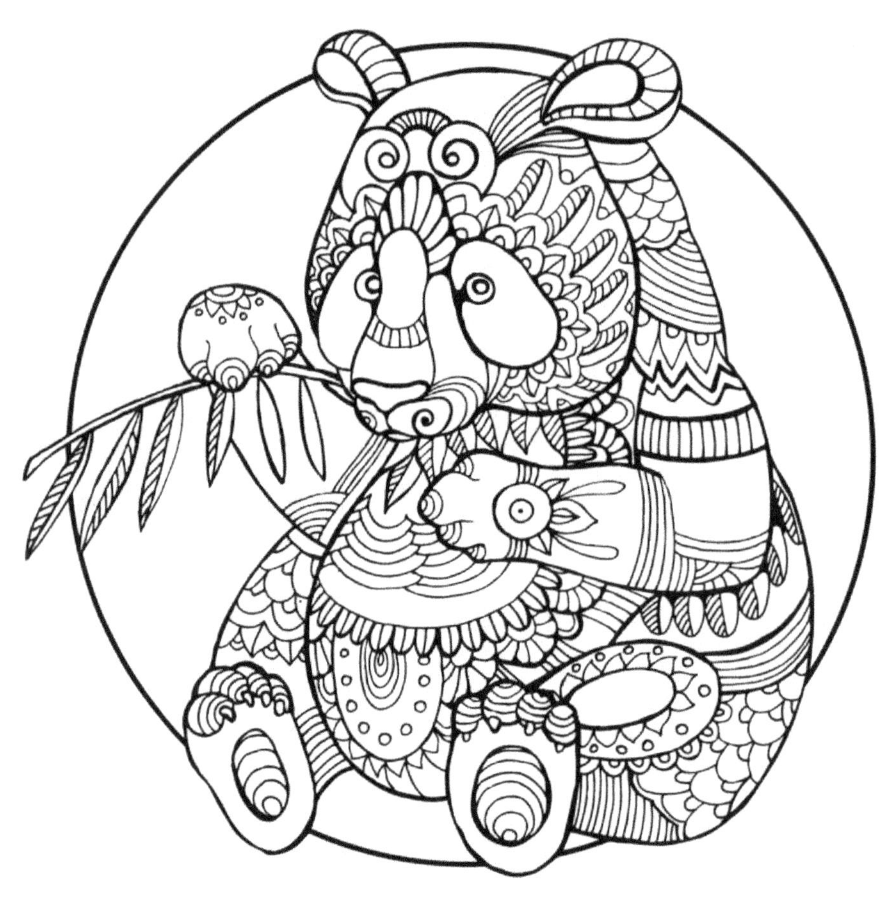

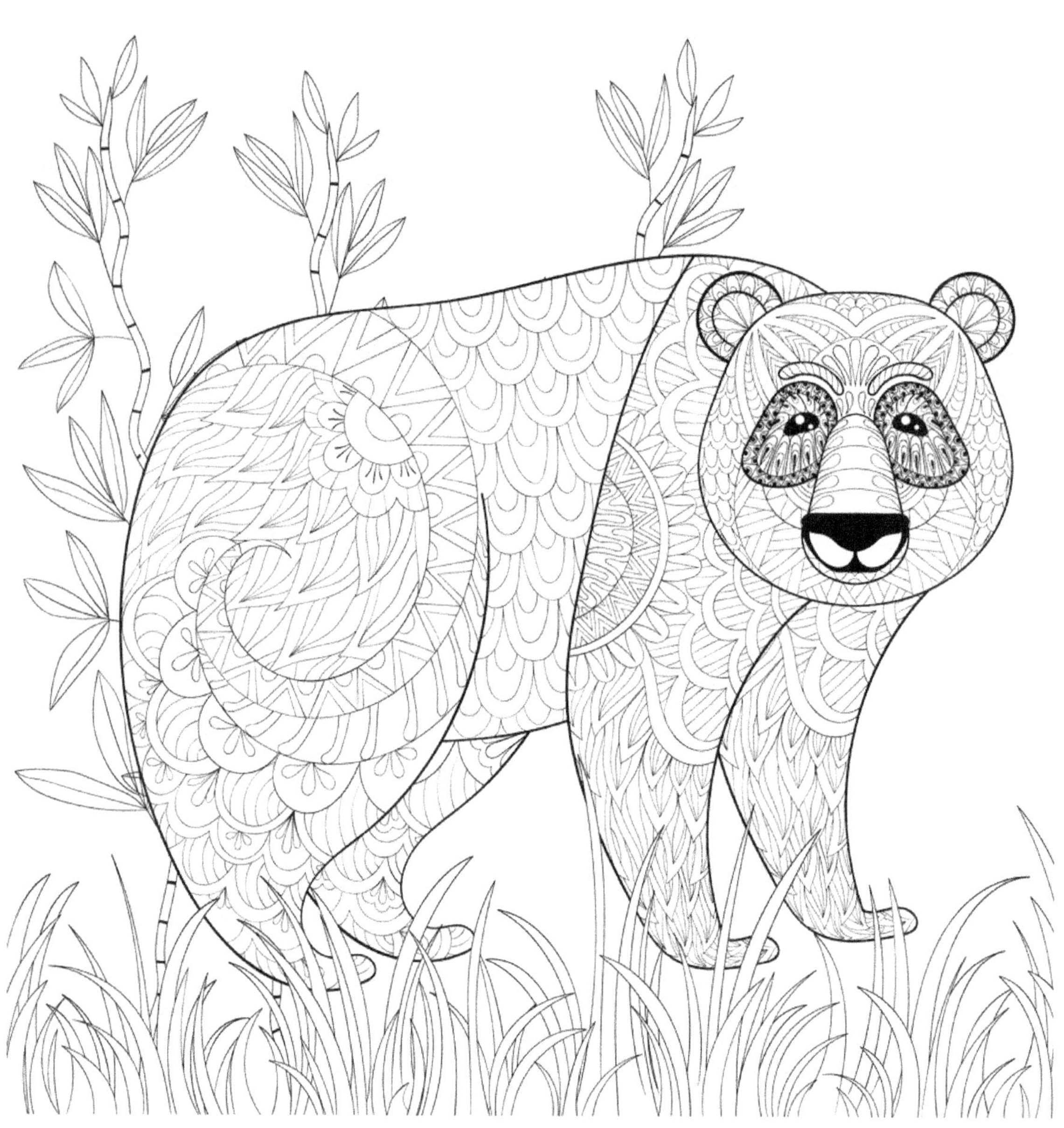

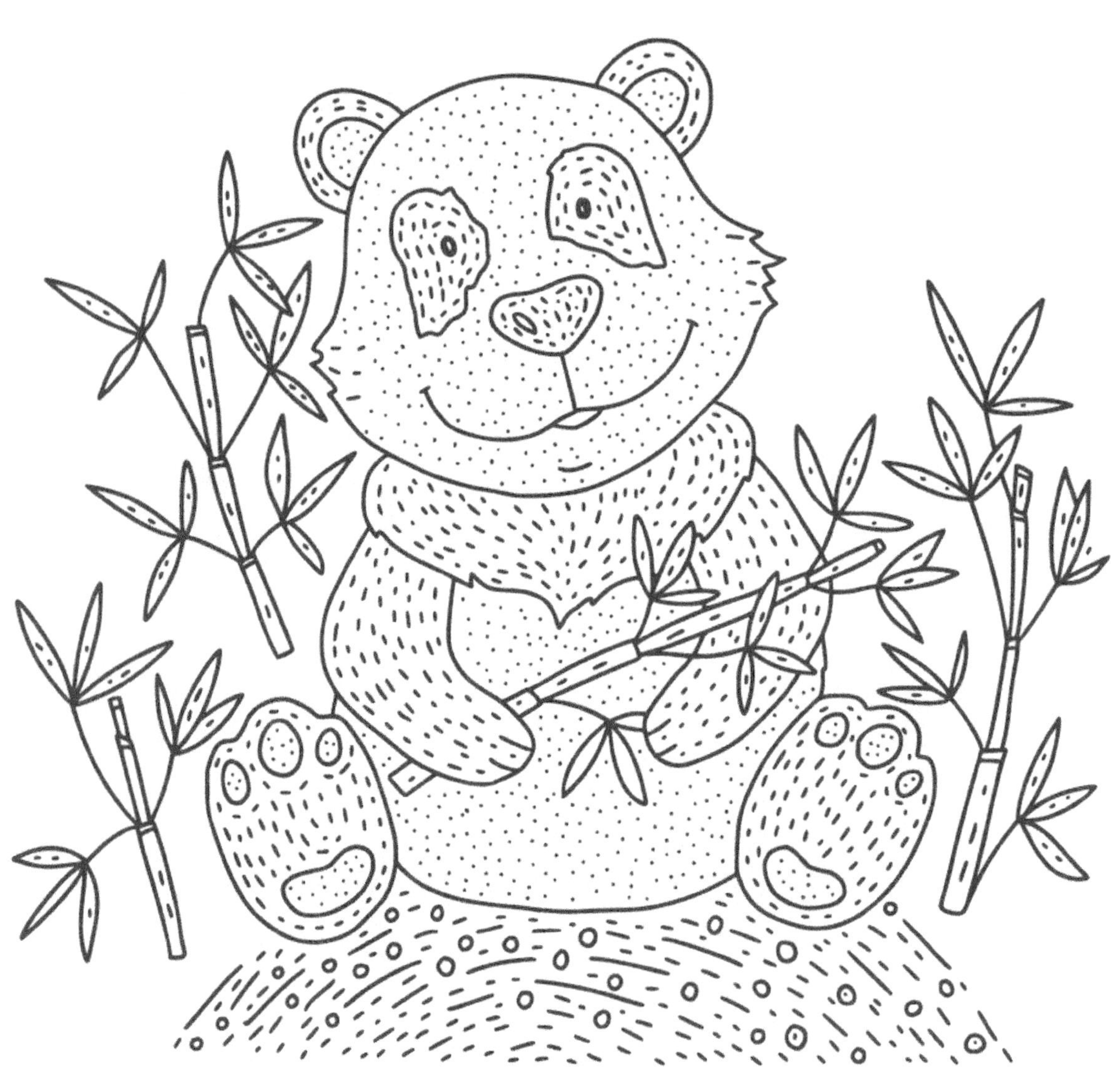

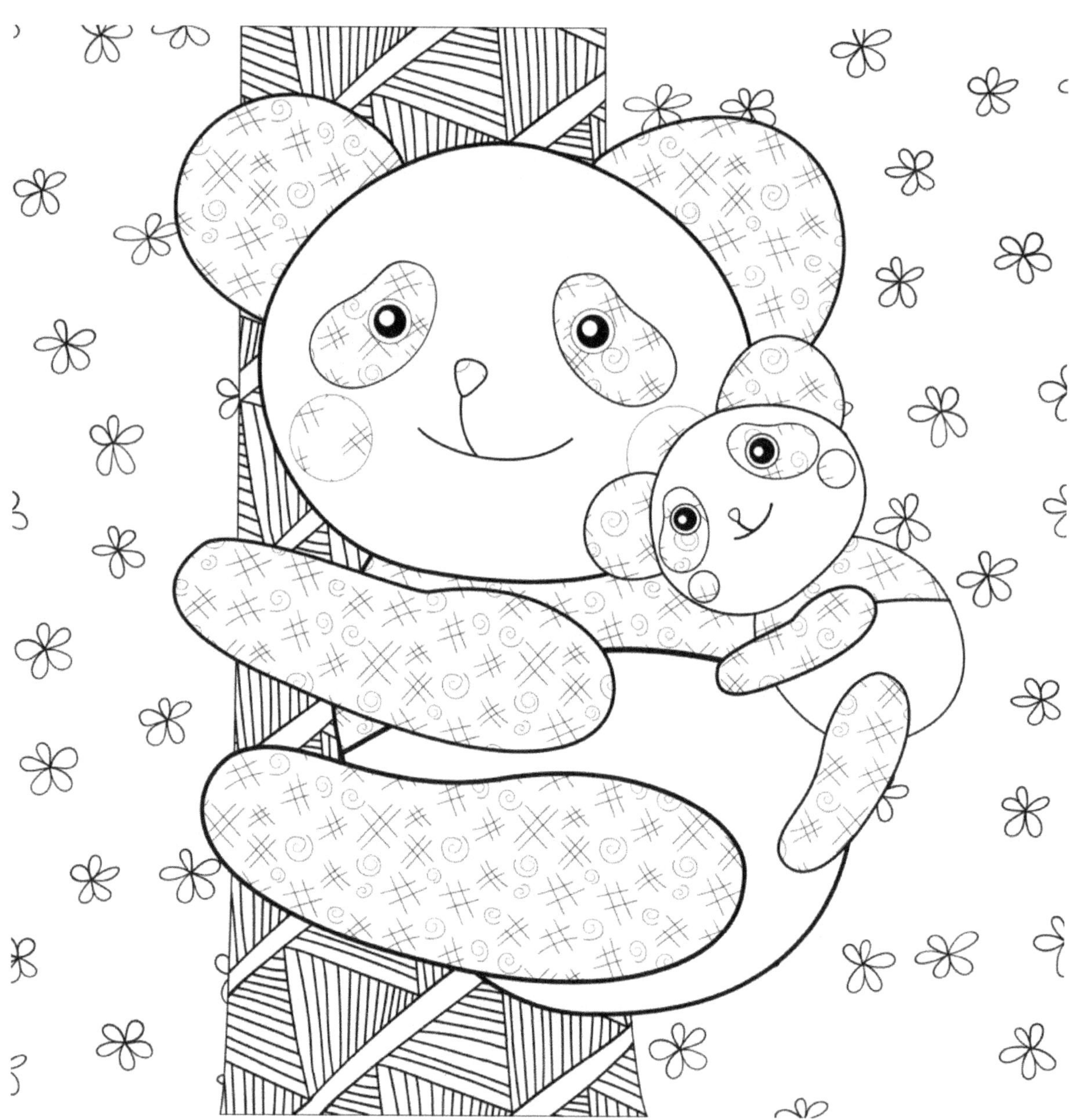

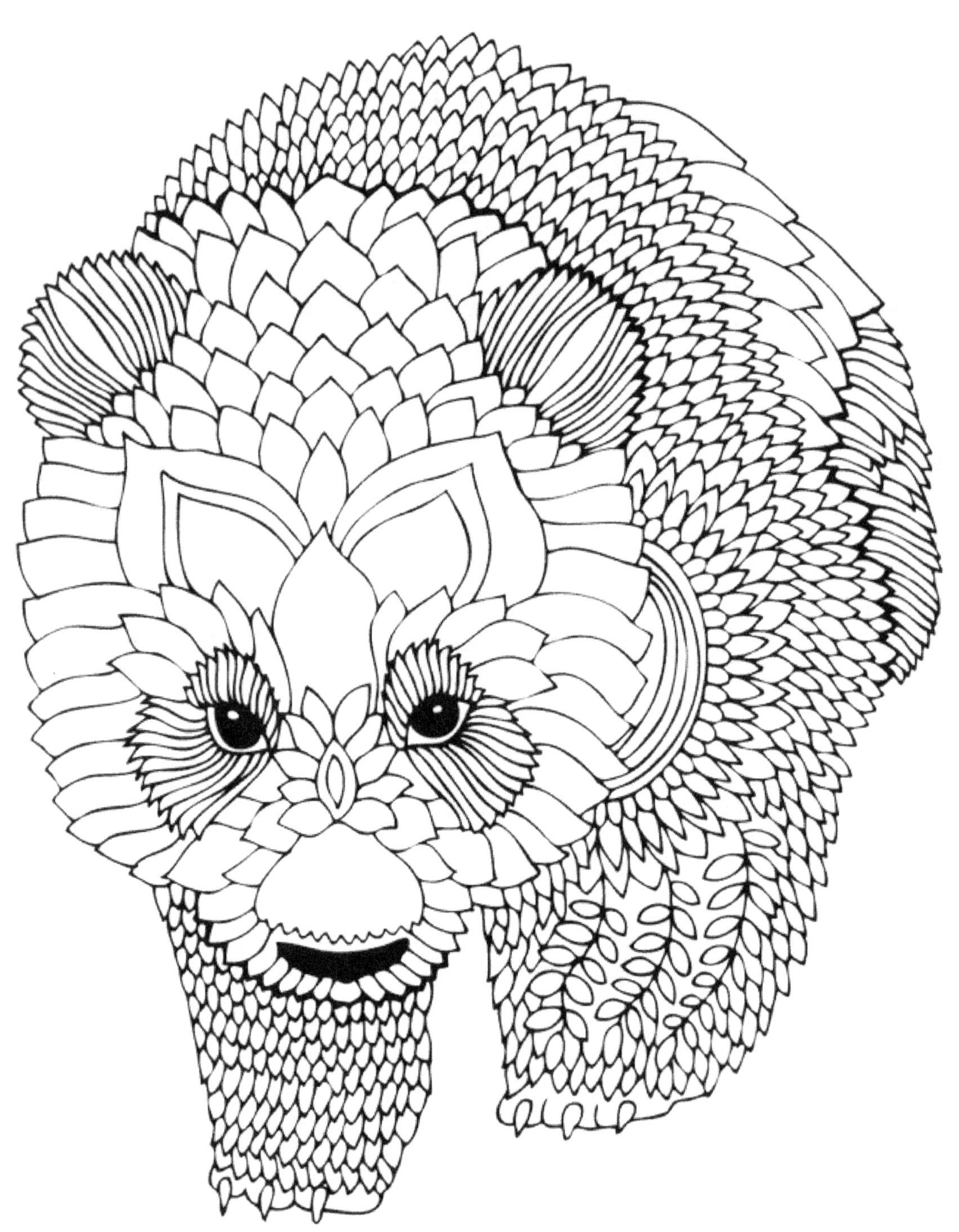

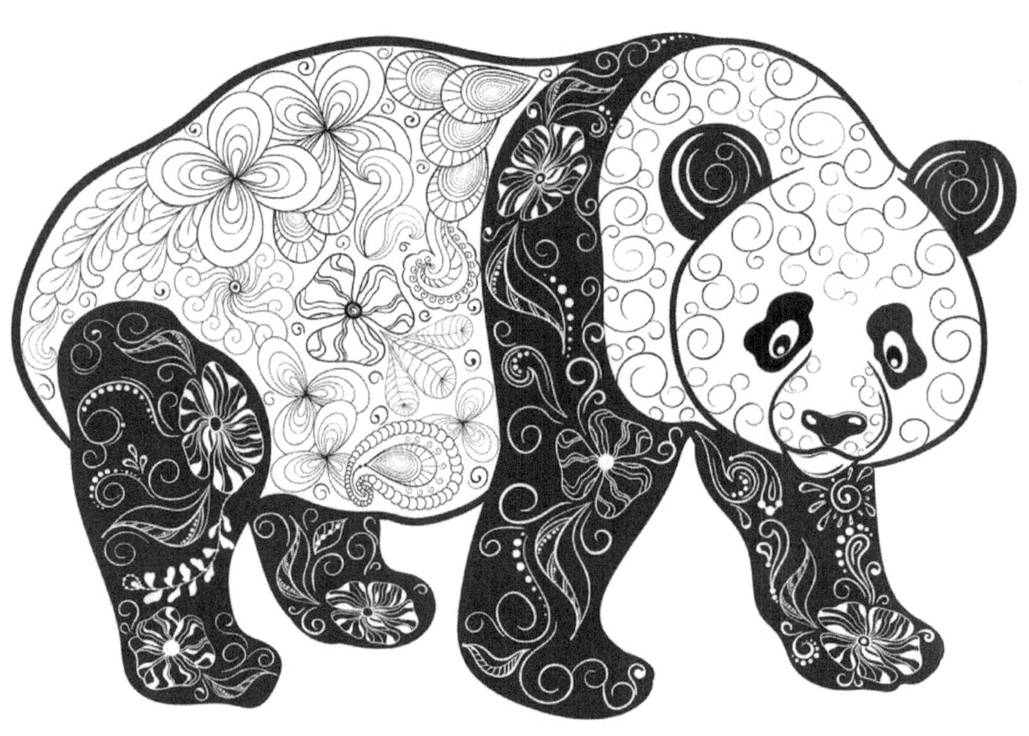

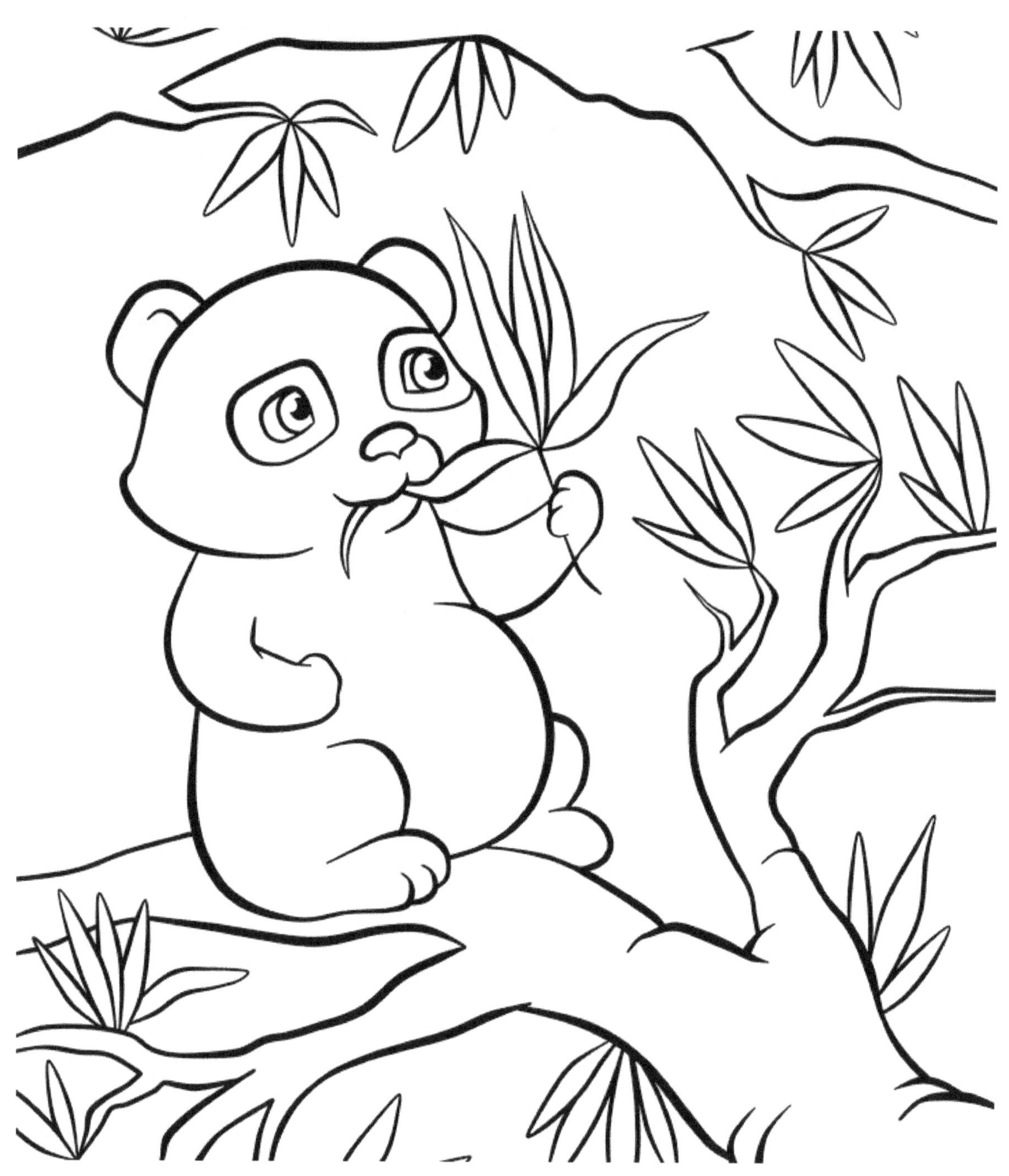

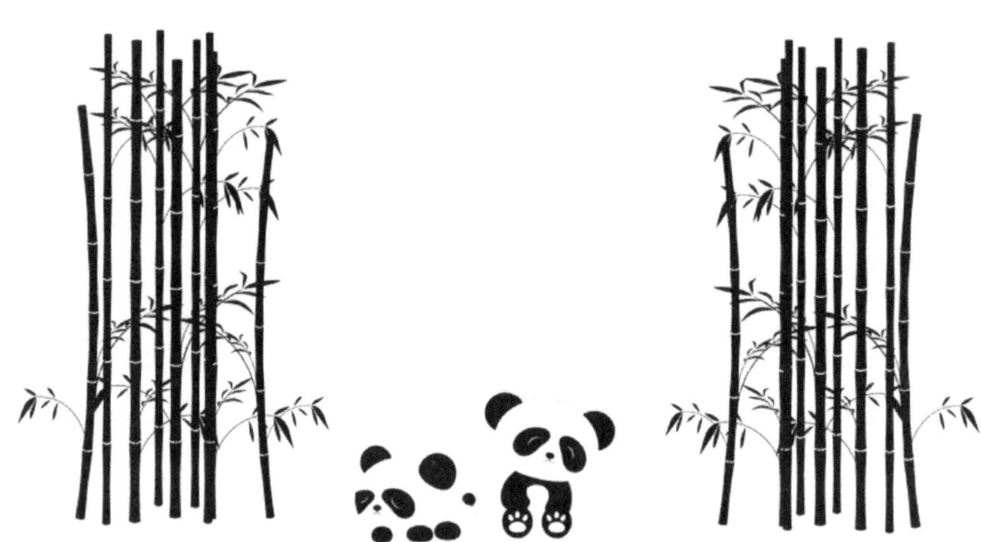

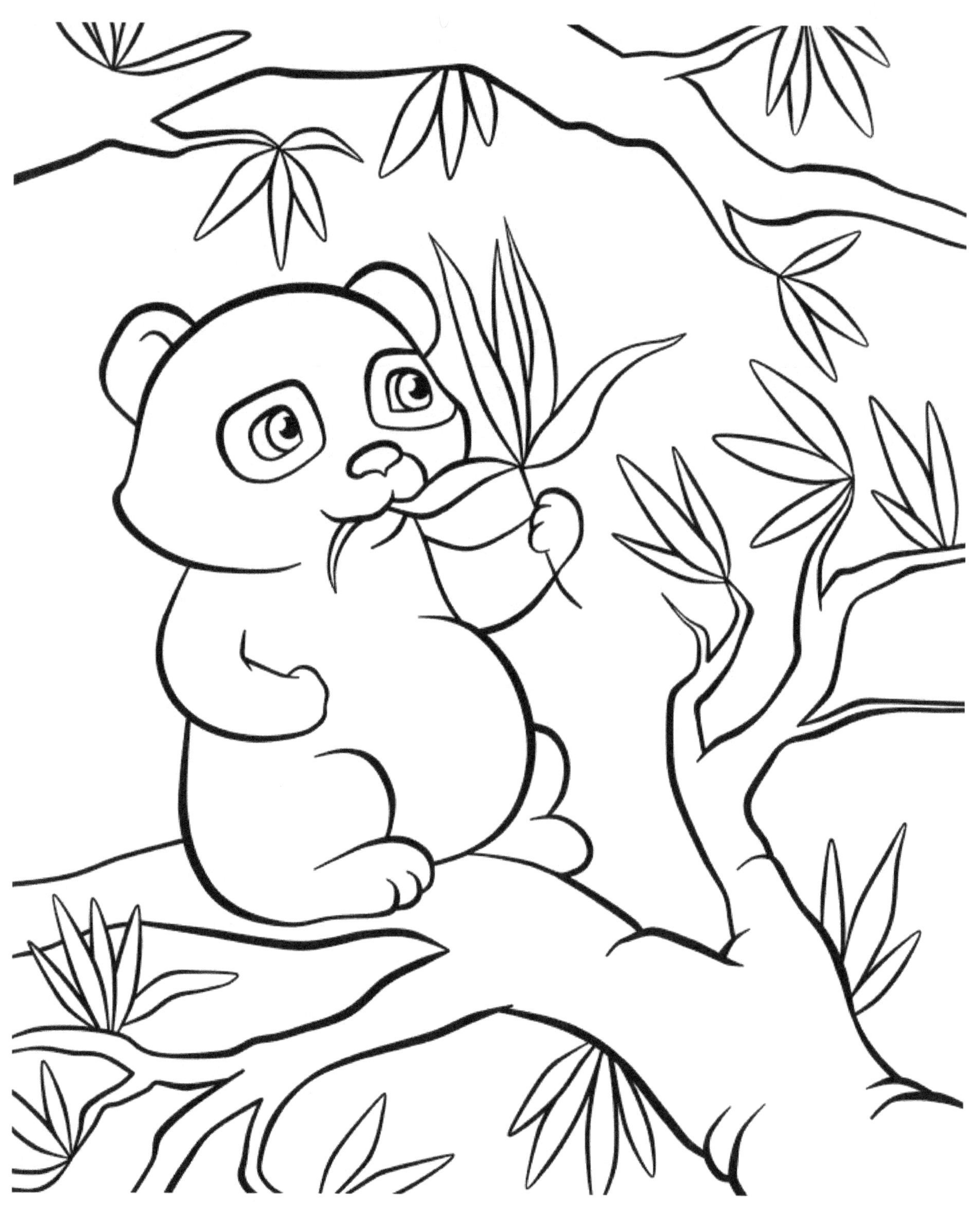

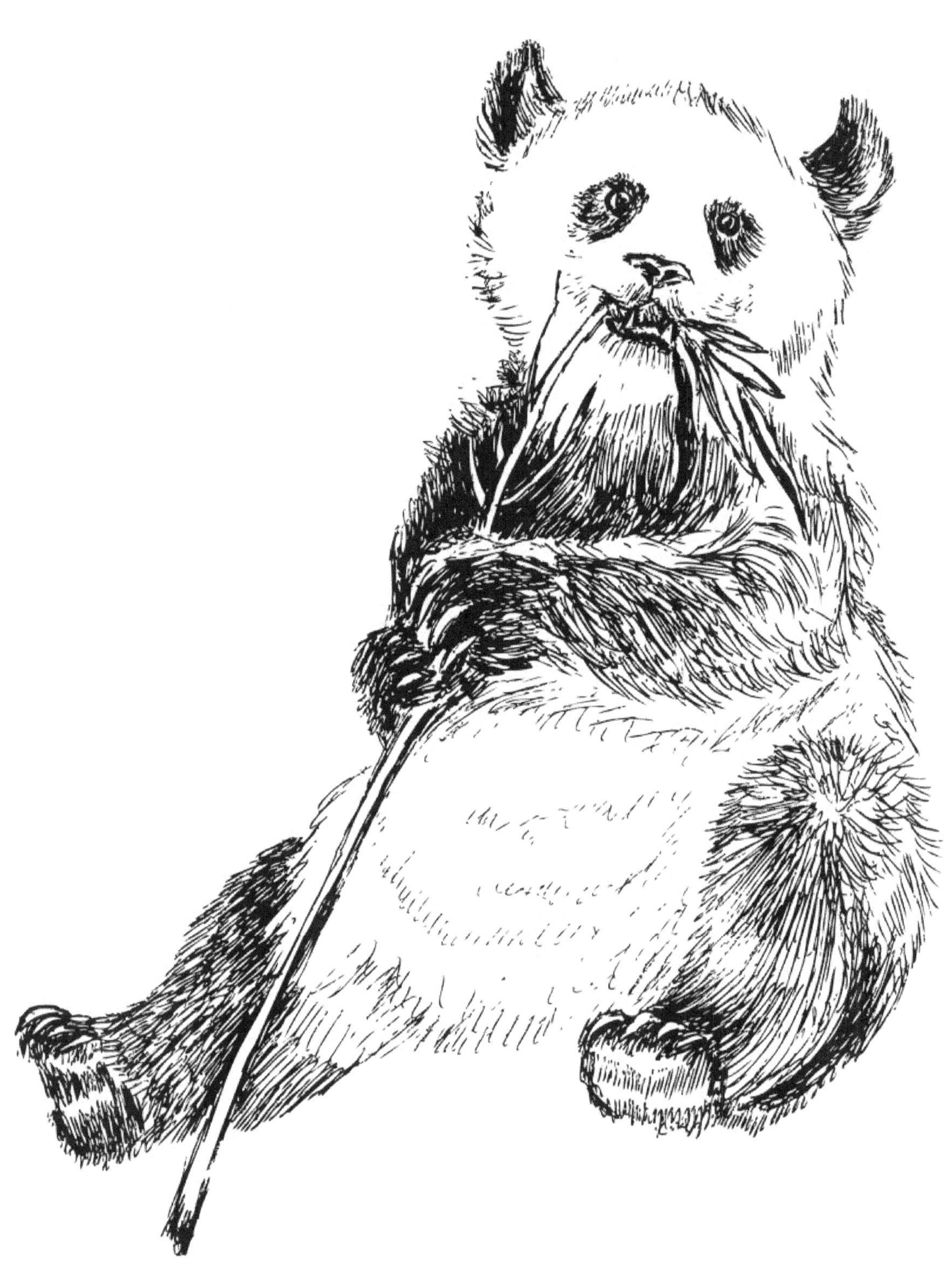

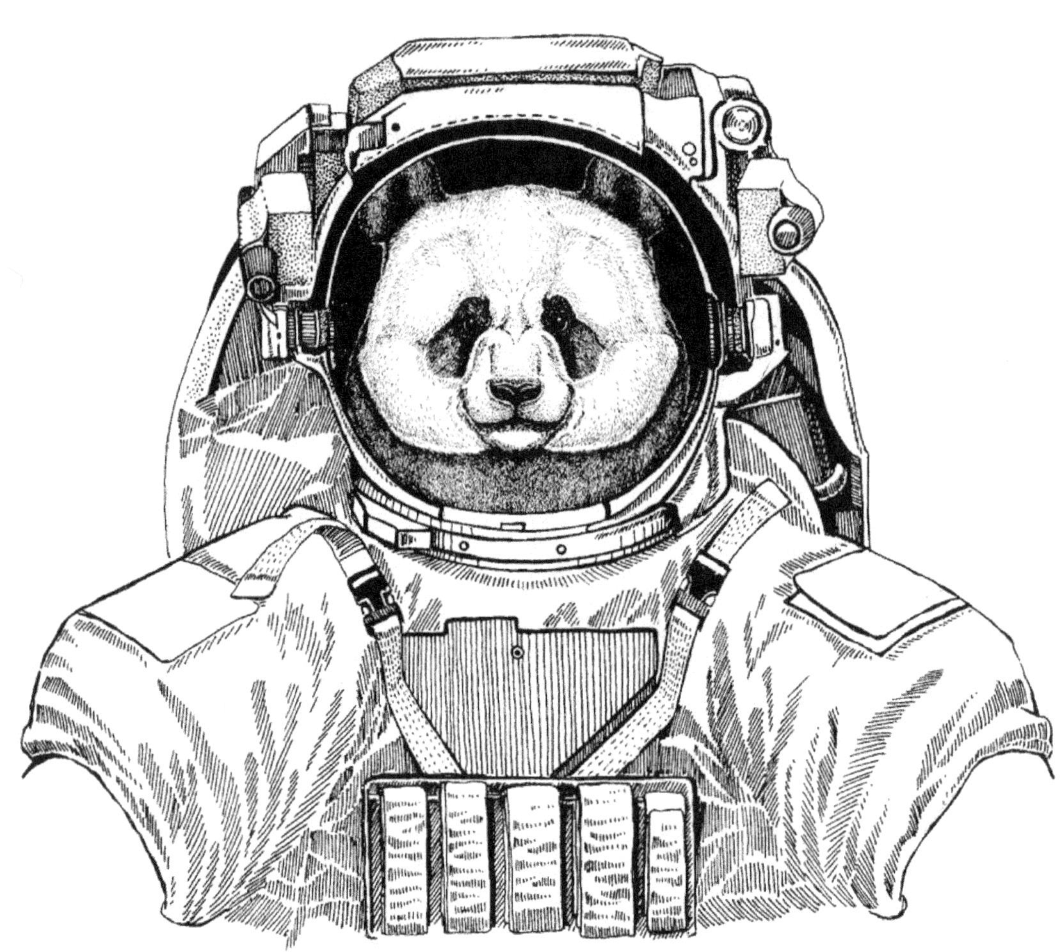

I need more Space

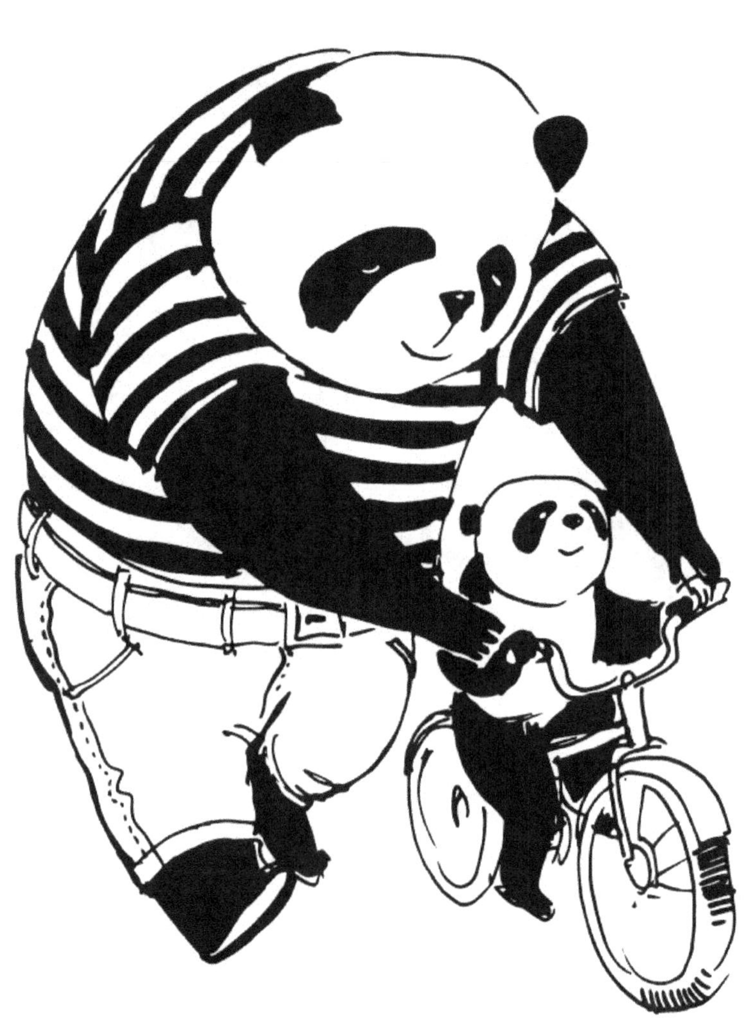

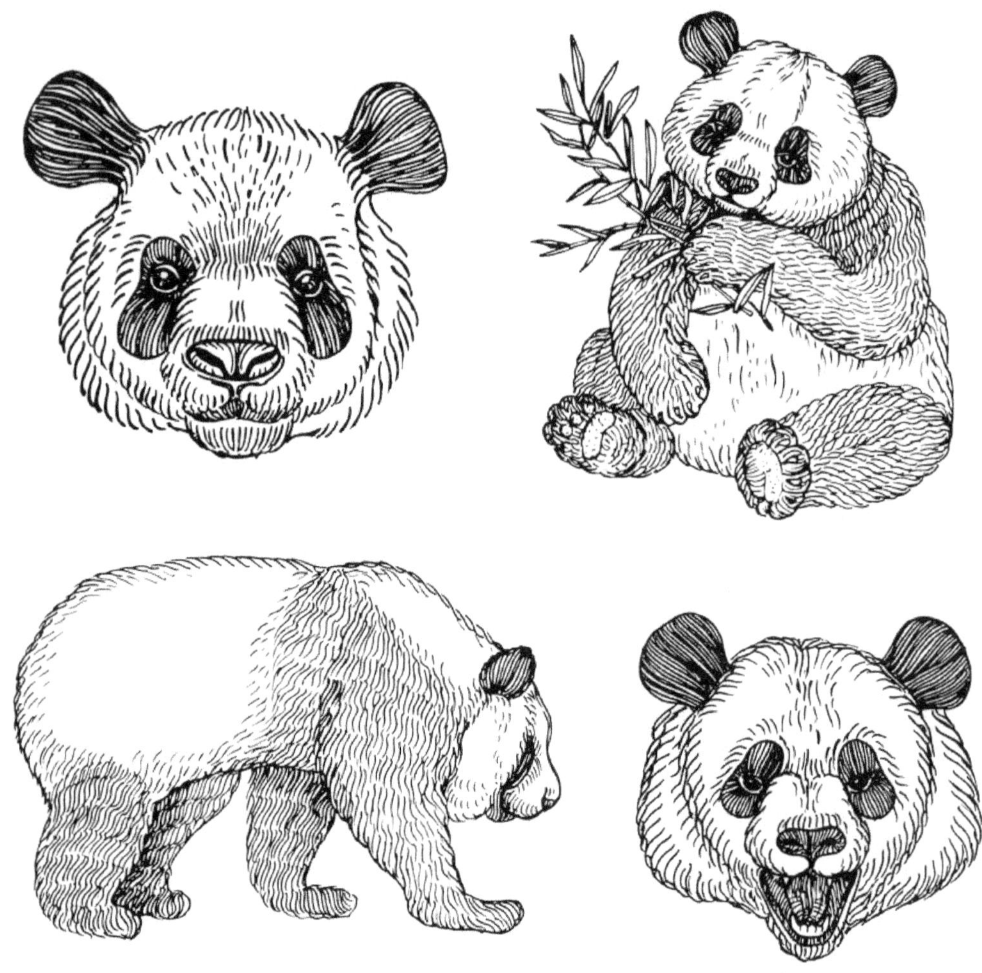

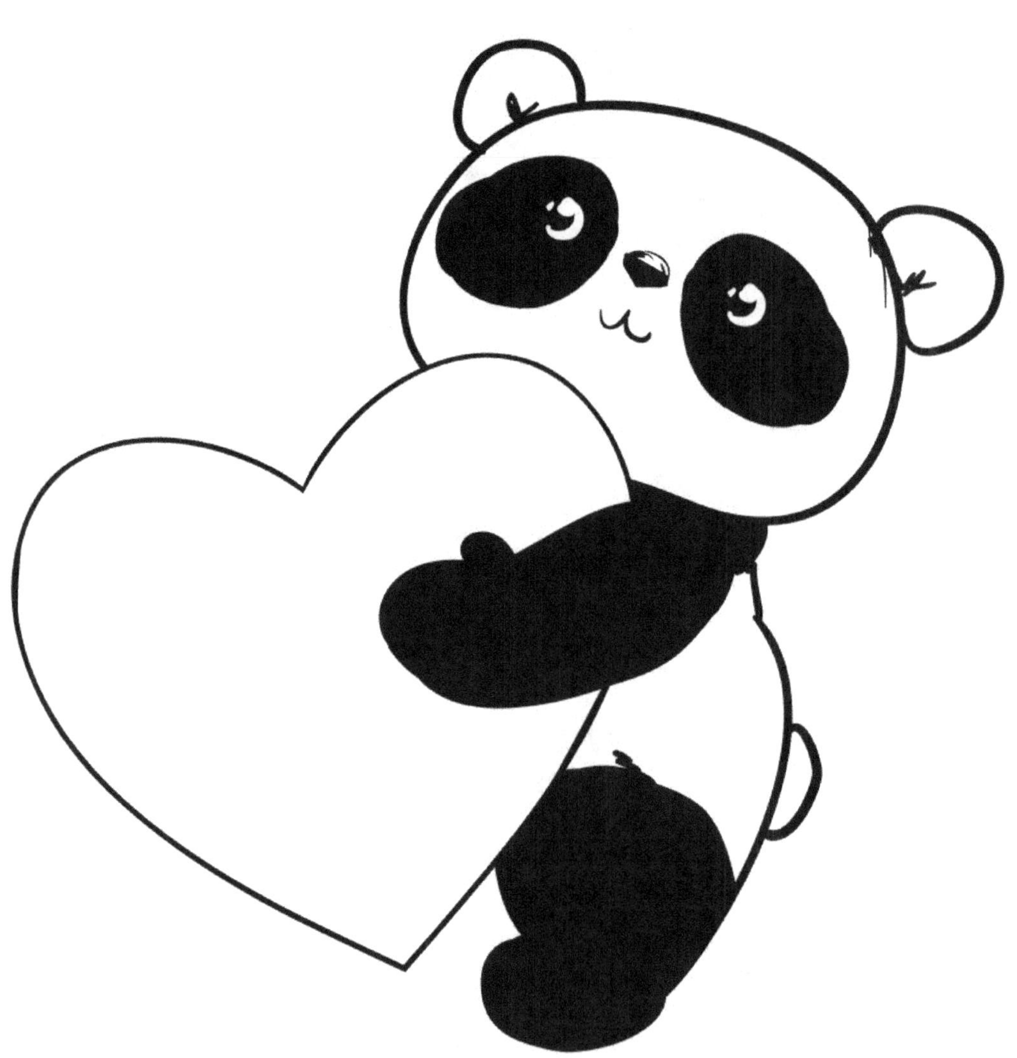

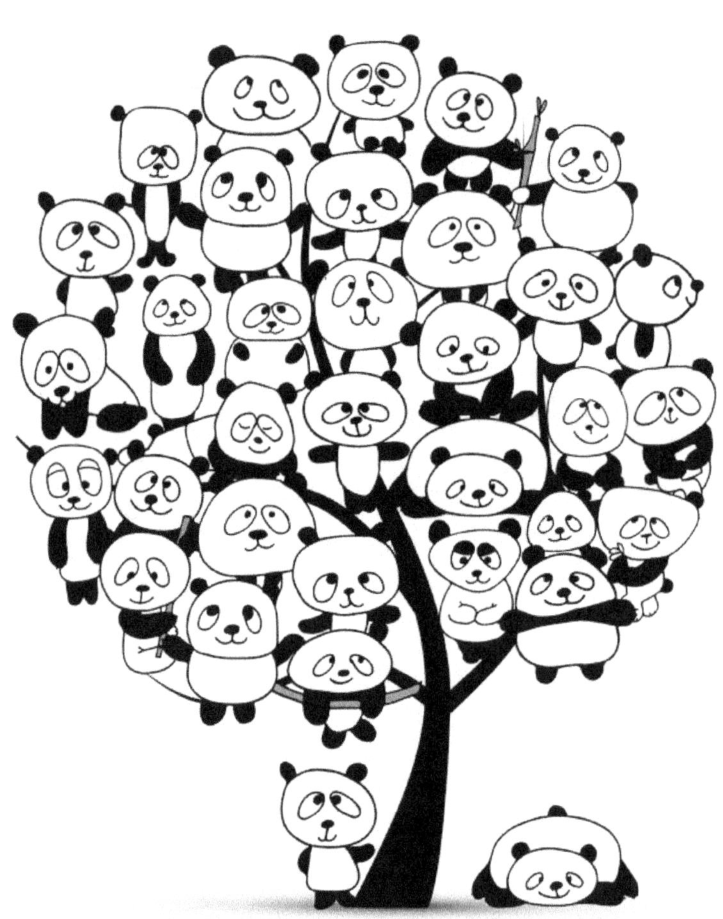

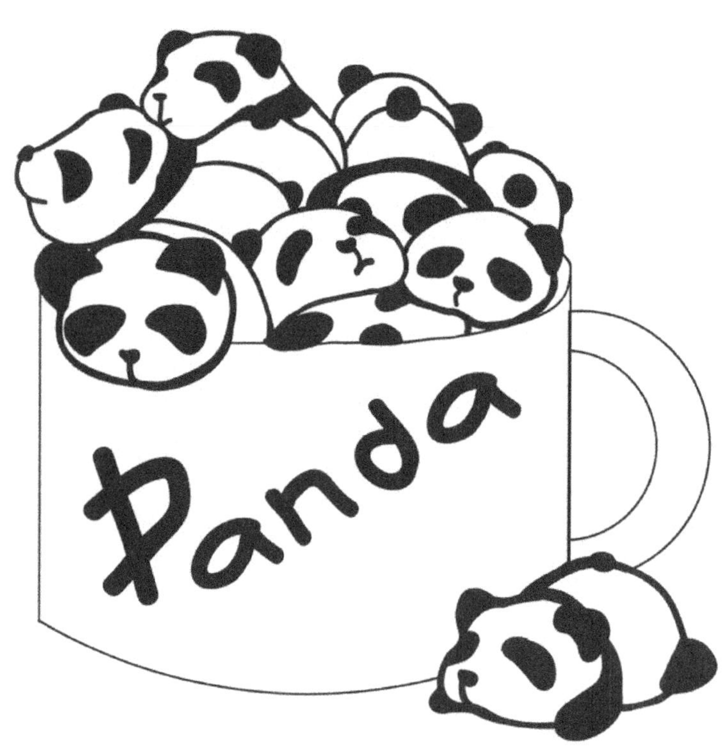

Panda

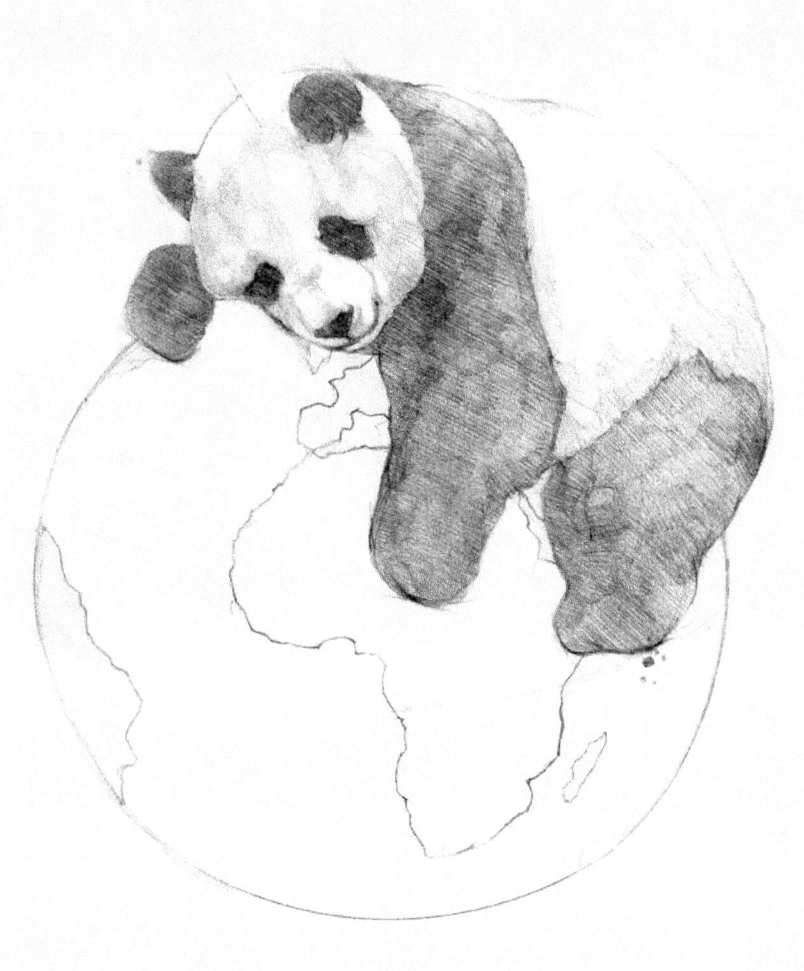

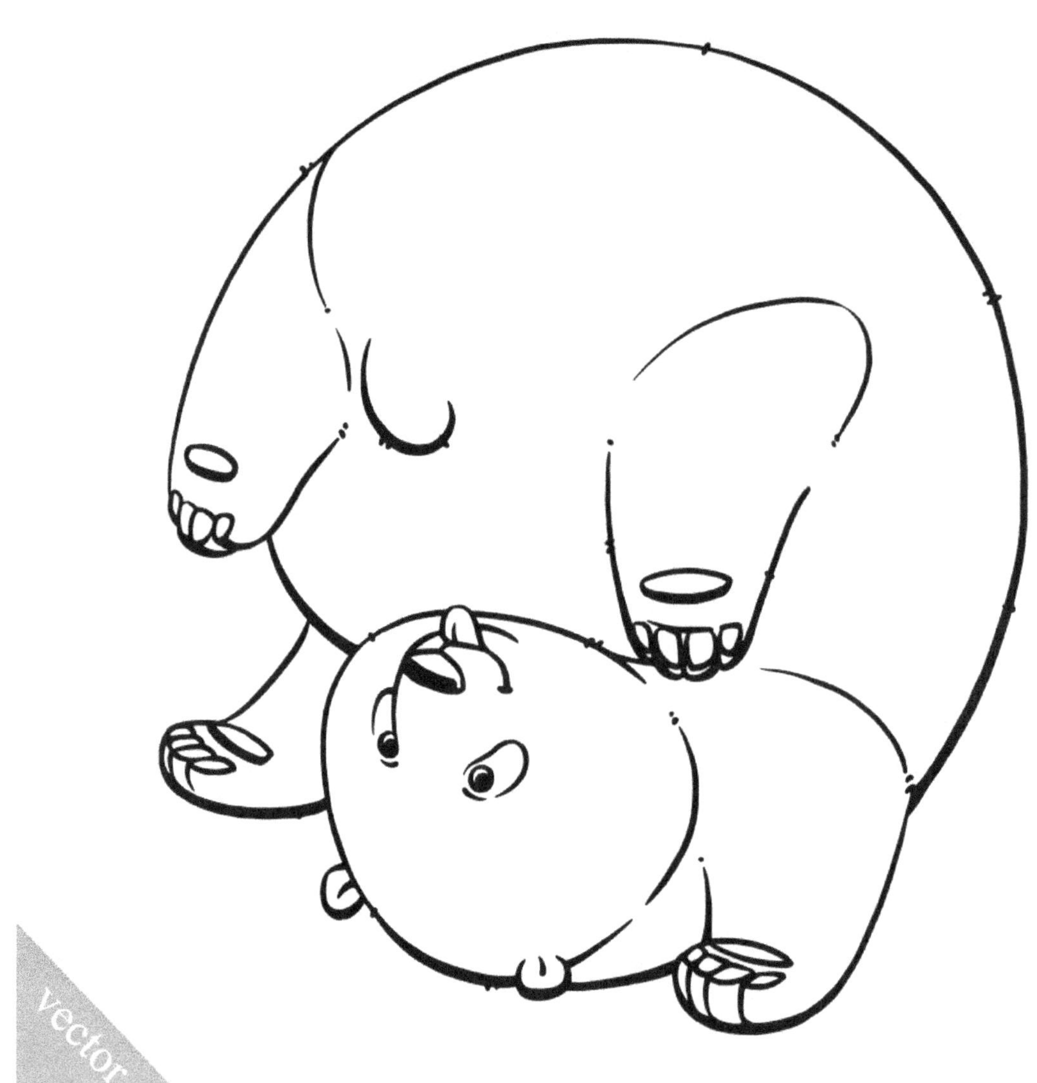

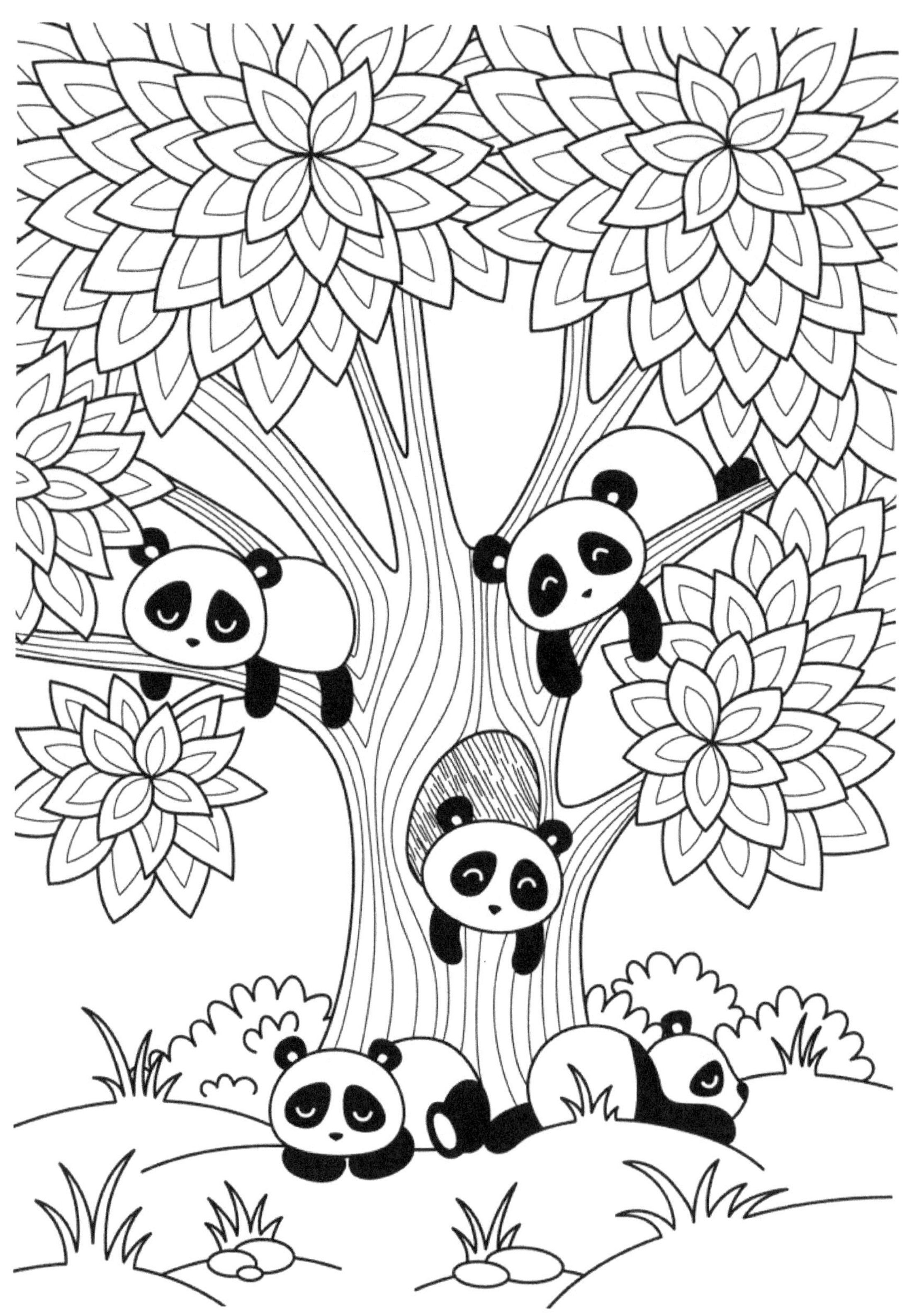

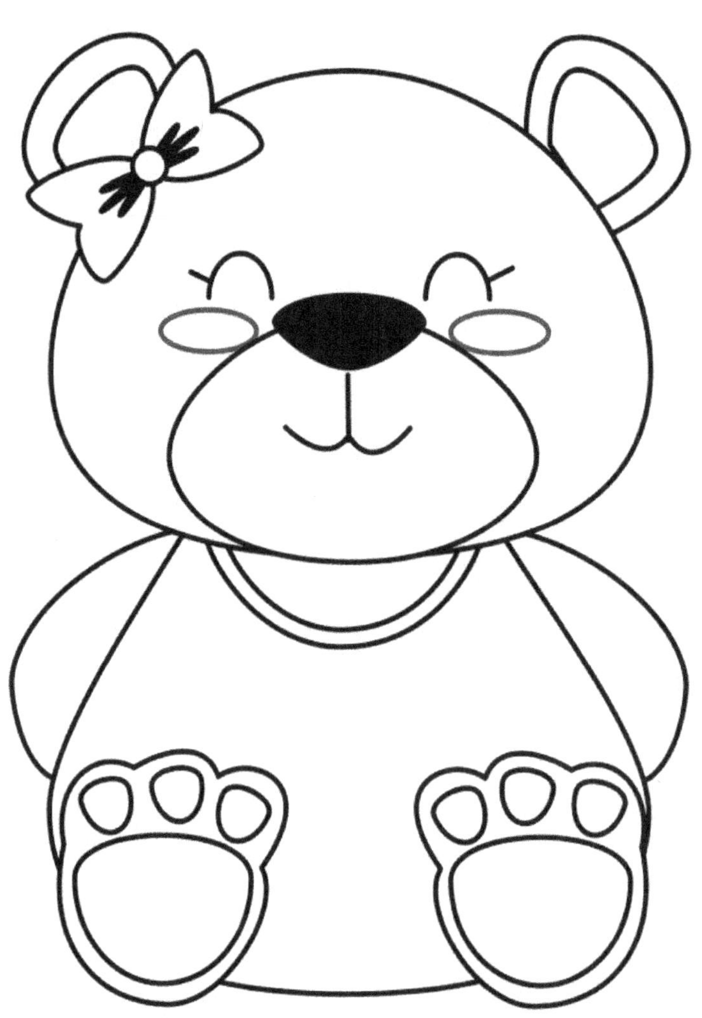

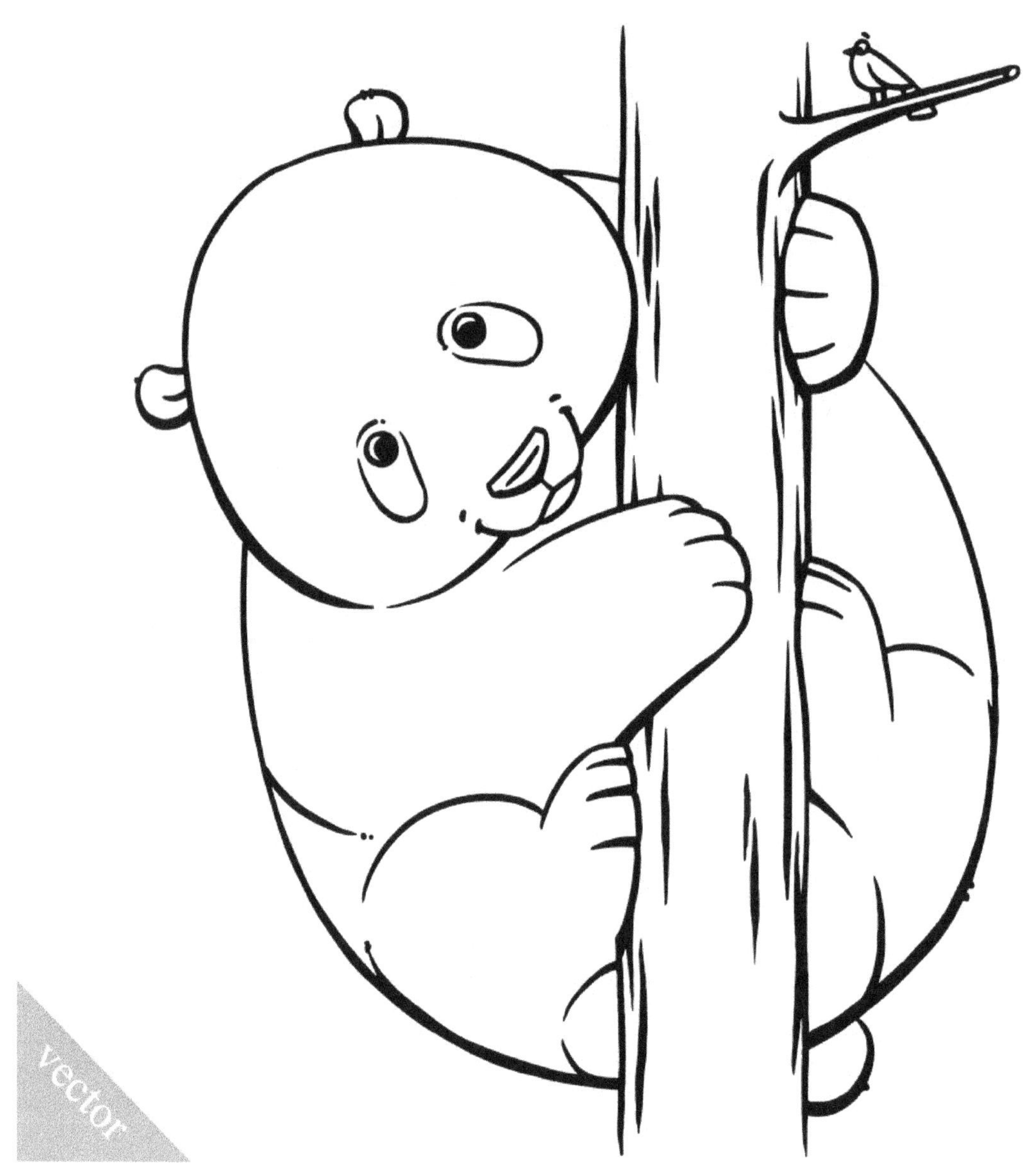

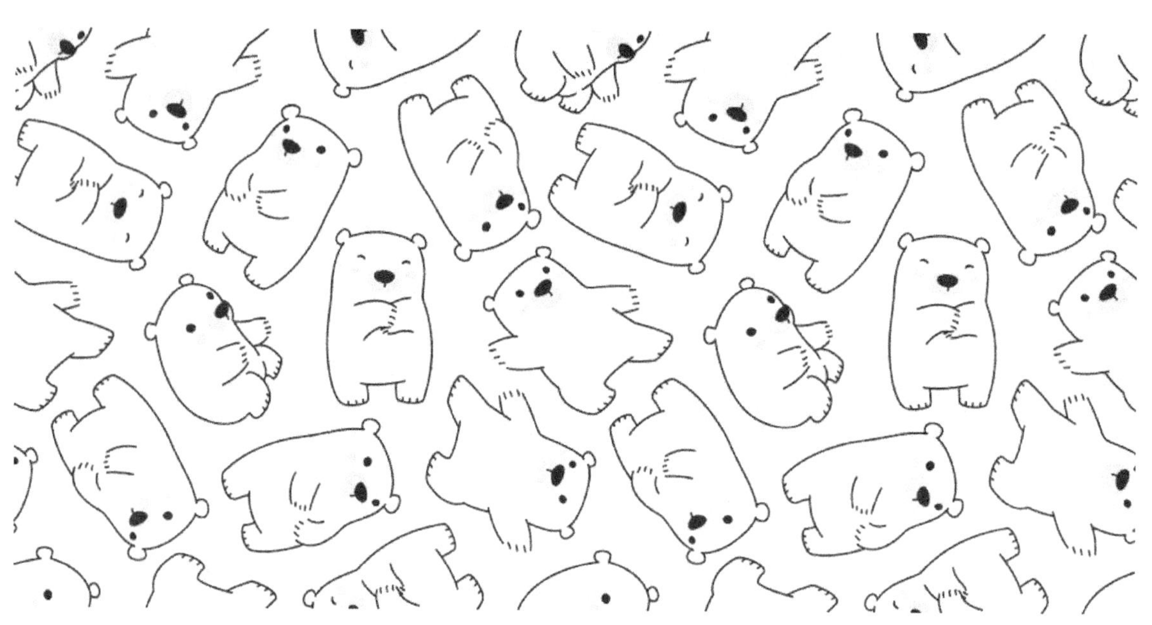

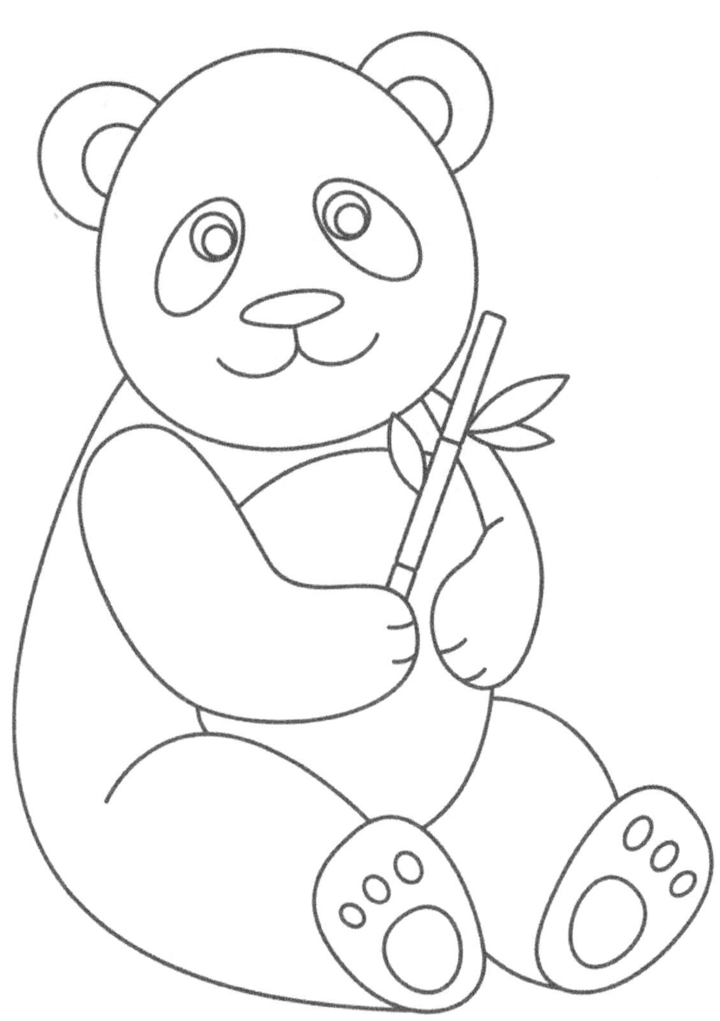

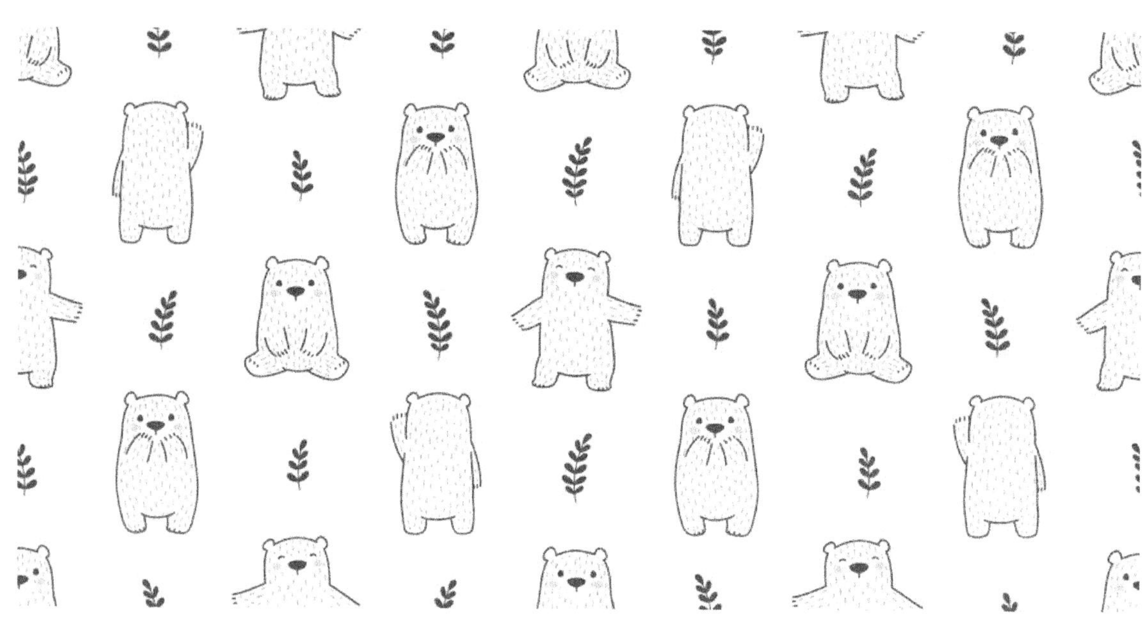

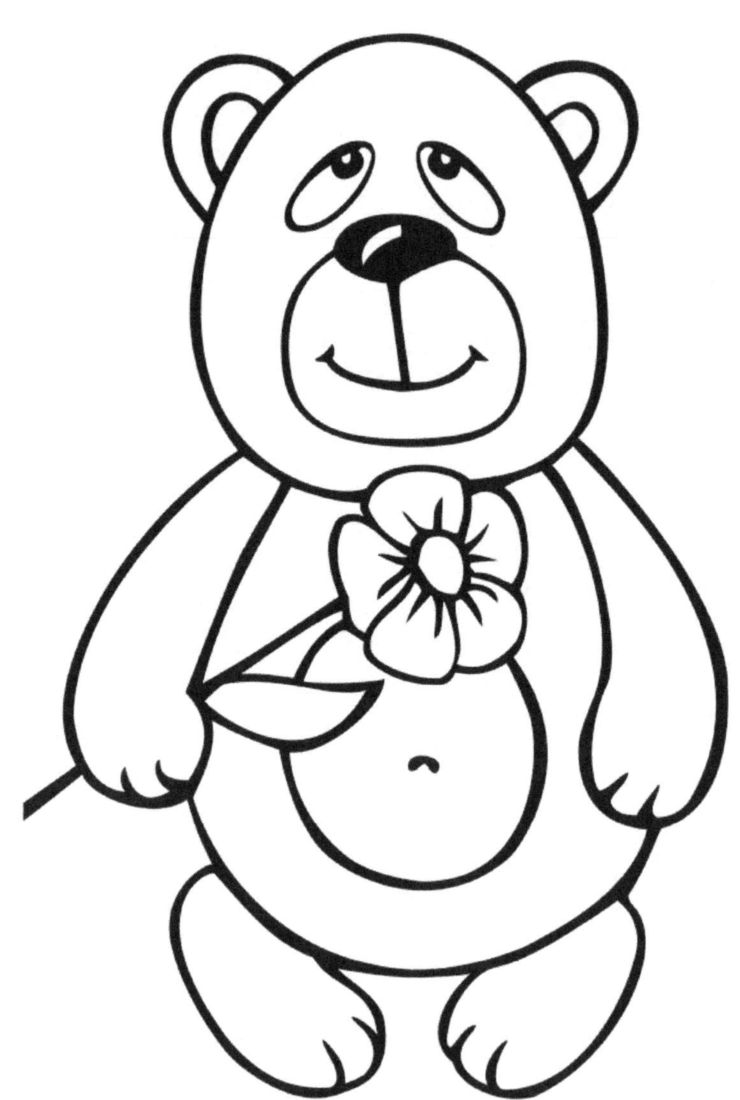

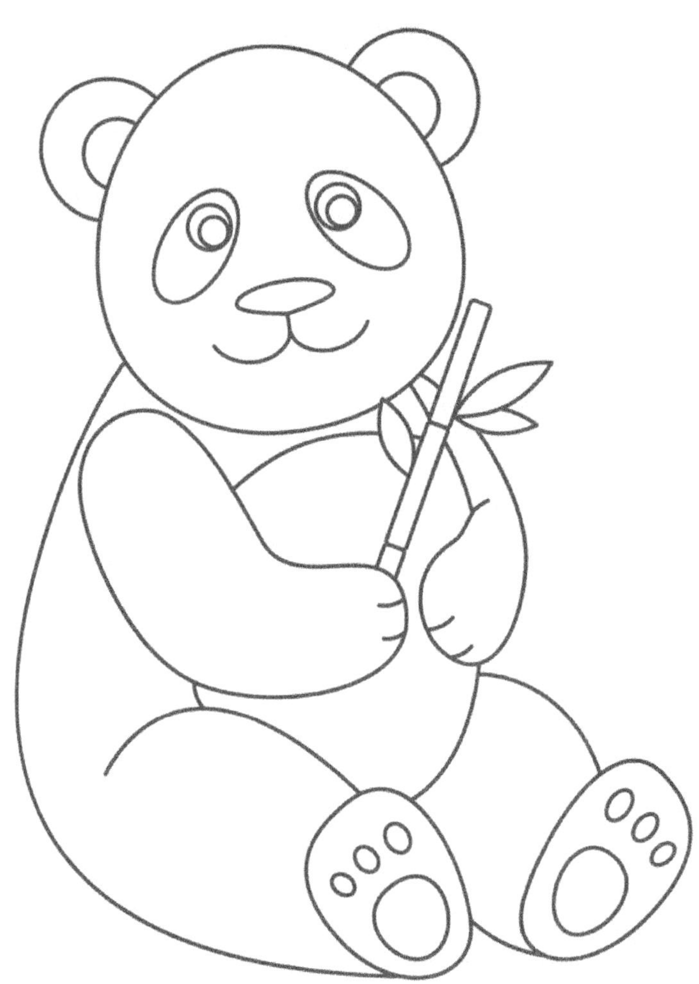

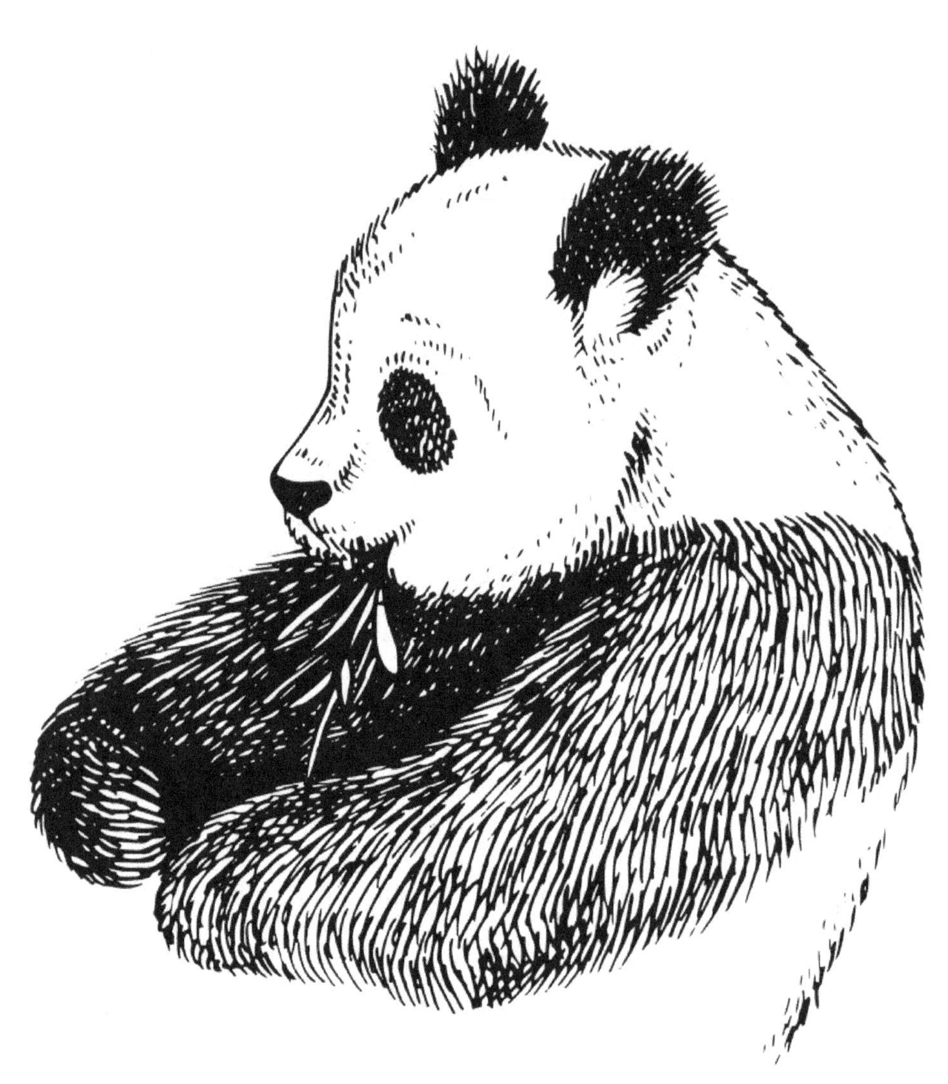

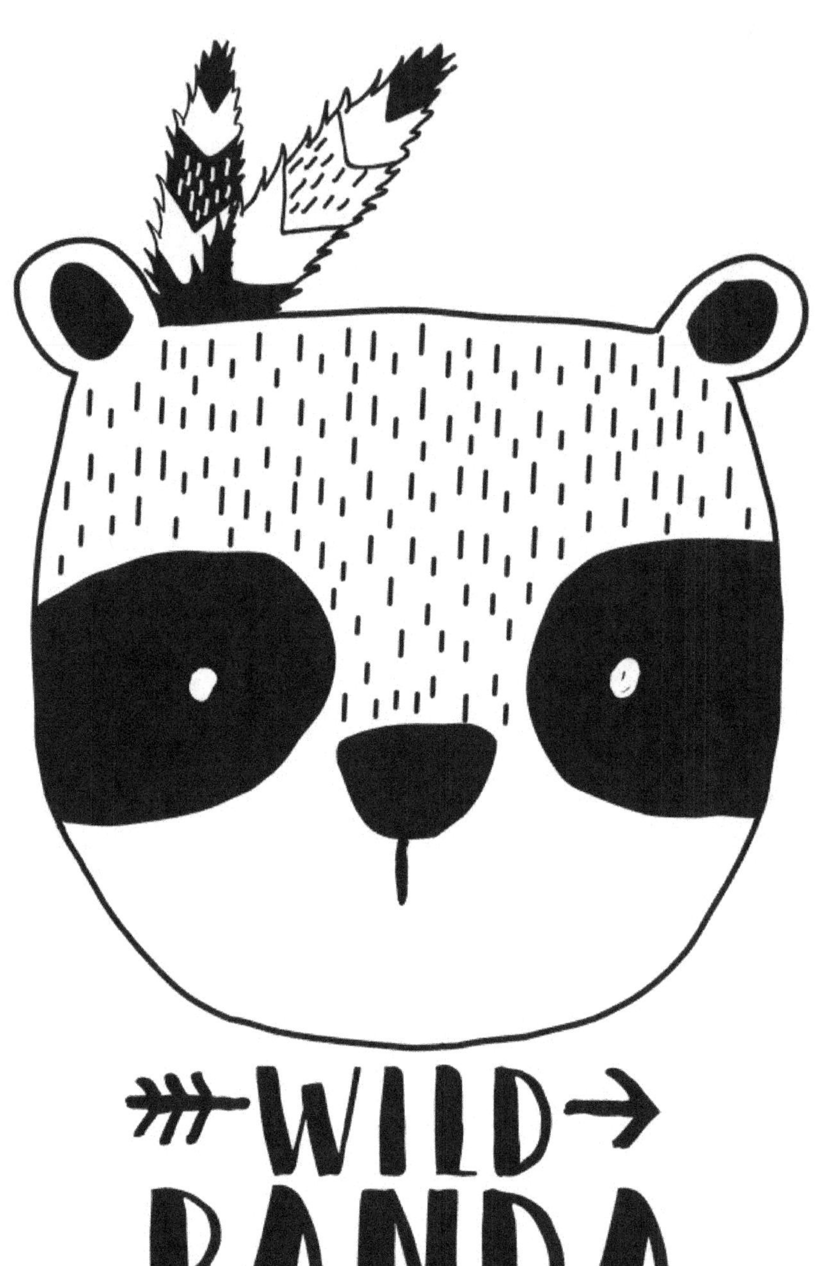

WILD
PANDA

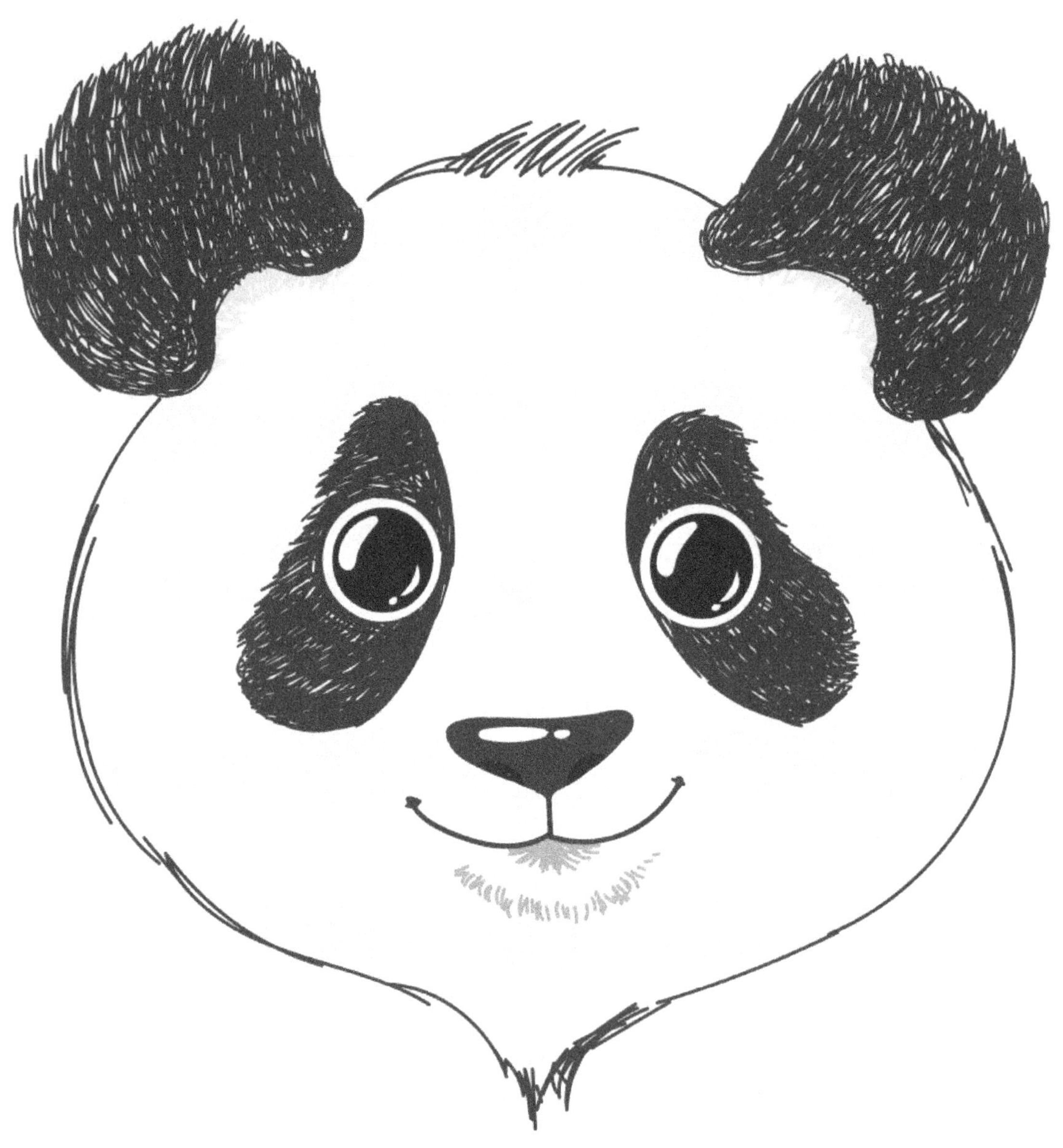

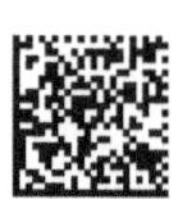

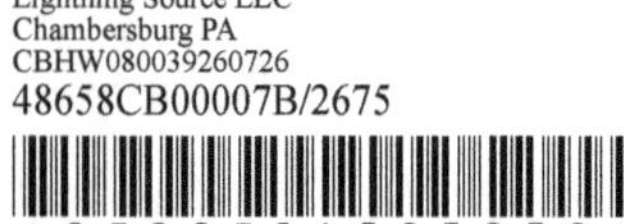
9 798724 593038